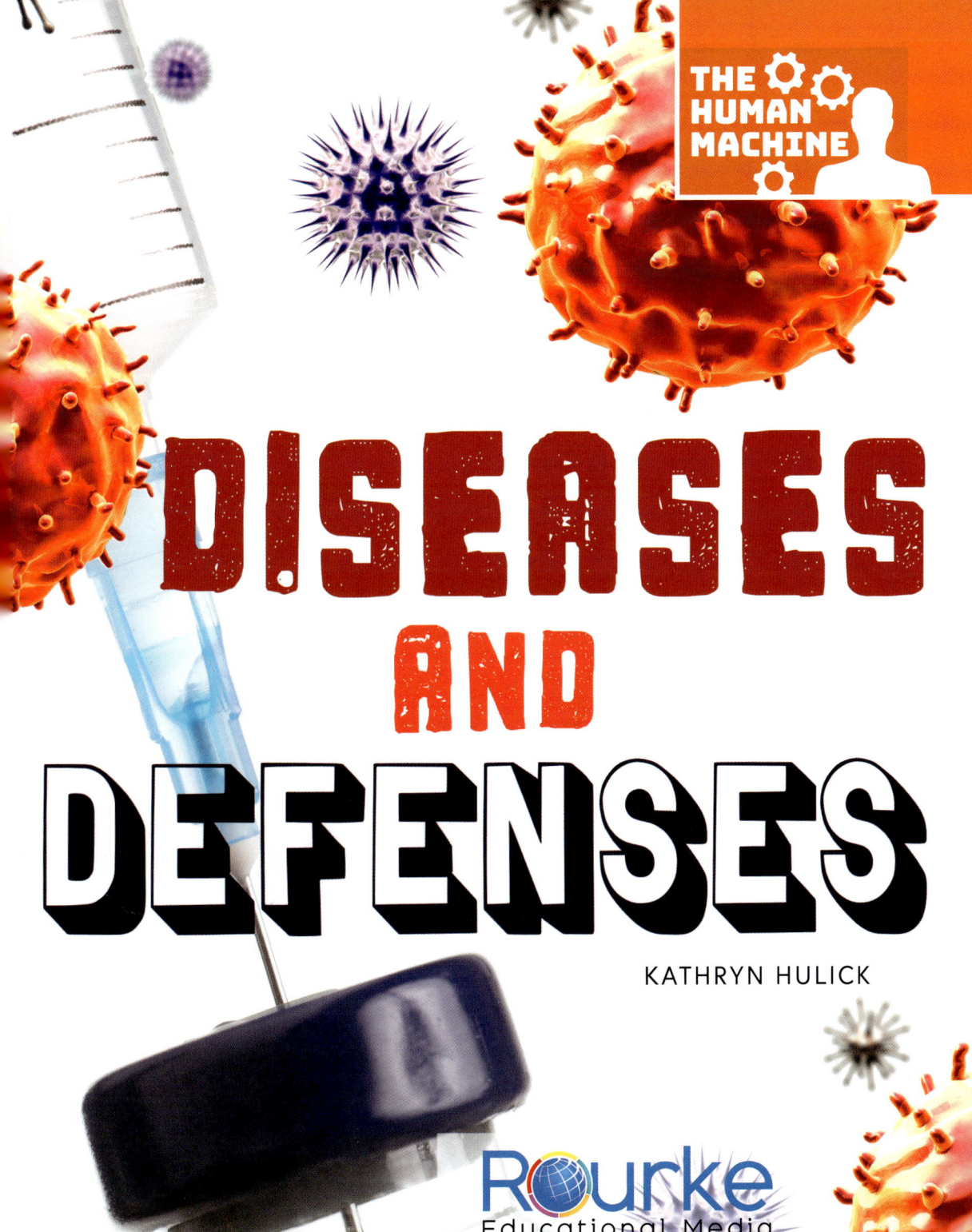

Before & After Reading Activities

Before Reading:

Building Academic Vocabulary and Background Knowledge

Before reading a book, it is important to tap into what your child or students already know about the topic. This will help them develop their vocabulary, increase their reading comprehension, and make connections across the curriculum.

1. Look at the cover of the book. What will this book be about?
2. What do you already know about the topic?
3. Let's study the Table of Contents. What will you learn about in the book's chapters?
4. What would you like to learn about this topic? Do you think you might learn about it from this book? Why or why not?
5. Use a reading journal to write about your knowledge of this topic. Record what you already know about the topic and what you hope to learn about the topic.
6. Read the book.
7. In your reading journal, record what you learned about the topic and your response to the book.
8. After reading the book complete the activities below.

Content Area Vocabulary

Read the list. What do these words mean?

addiction
antibiotics
antibodies
contagious
genes
germs
immune system
infections
inflammation
microbes
probiotics

After Reading:

Comprehension and Extension Activity

After reading the book, work on the following questions with your child or students in order to check their level of reading comprehension and content mastery.

1. How does the immune system protect the body? (Summarize)
2. How might probiotics help cure a disease? (Infer)
3. Why do some people have allergies? (Asking Questions)
4. The last time you felt sick, how did your body respond? (Text to Self Connection)
5. How does getting old affect the body's health? (Asking Questions)

Extension Activity

Pick a disease that has affected a person in your family. How did the disease happen? Was it the result of genes, lifestyle, or an infection? Research treatments for the disease. Pretend that you are a doctor, and a friend is a patient with the disease. Explain the disease and its treatments to them.

TABLE OF CONTENTS

A Broken Machine	4
Tiny Soldiers in the Blood	8
Meet the Invaders	14
Helpful Microbes	18
Living a Healthy Life	20
Cancer	26
Glossary	30
Index	31
Show What You Know	31
Further Reading	31
About the Author	32

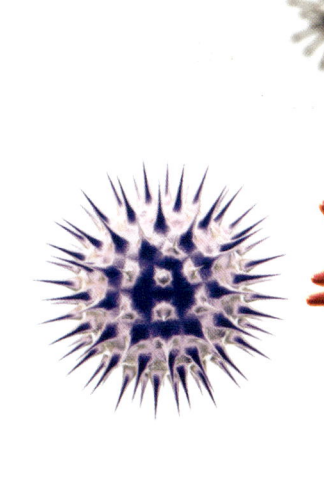
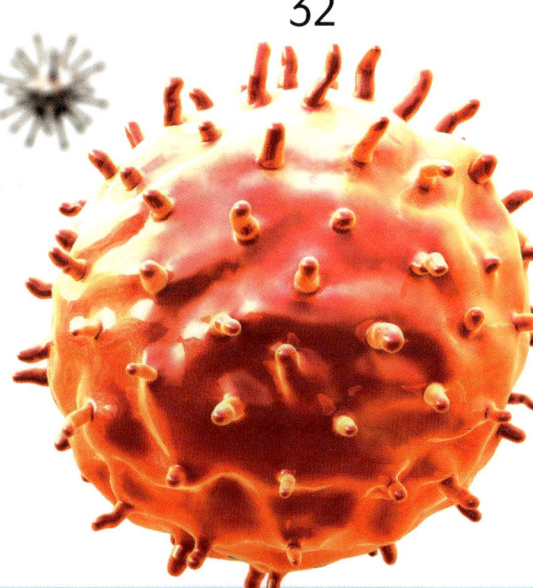

A BROKEN MACHINE

How are you feeling? Are you healthy? That means your body is working properly. The body is like a machine. It runs on food, water, and air. Its systems let you think, feel, move, and experience the world.

But the world is full of dangers. Falls, burns, and other accidents lead to injury. **Germs** surround us at all times. These tiny invaders may make people sick. And sometimes body systems fail on their own.

A sick or injured body is like a broken machine. It needs repair. Thankfully, it can often fix itself. The **immune system** helps heal wounds and stop germs. A doctor or surgeon can also help a person feel better.

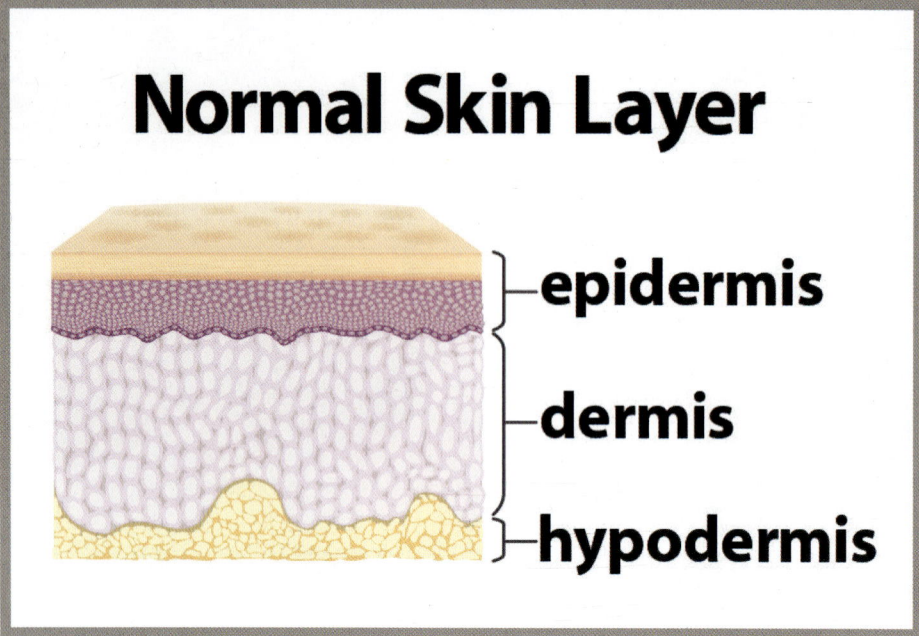

The skin is the immune system's first line of defense. Skin may not seem very special. It's no turtle shell. But the soft stretchy stuff that covers your body is quite tough.

The skin acts as armor against many dangers. Germs can't easily get through. Neither can harmful rays of sunlight. And skin rebuilds itself. It repairs small cuts and burns on its own.

Openings such as the eyes, nose, and mouth need their own defenses. Eyelashes and eyebrows keep dirt and germs out of the eyes. Snot, also called mucus, traps germs in the nose. Juices in the stomach destroy many germs that you swallow.

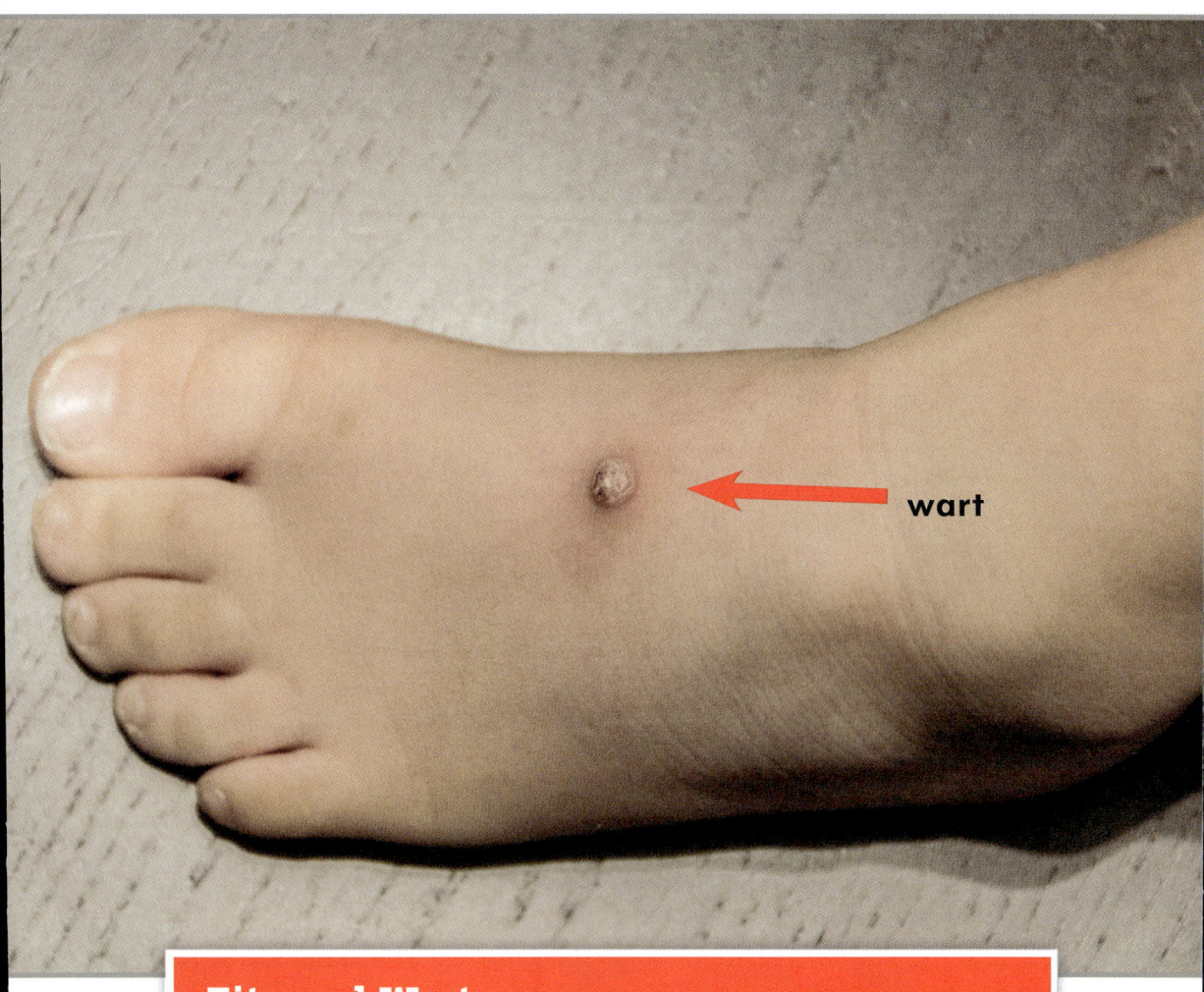

wart

Zits and Warts

You find a hard blob on your toe. Eww, a wart! Don't touch it or you might spread it to others. Zits are very different. Natural chemicals in teens' bodies are usually to blame. Zits don't spread from one person to another.

TINY SOLDIERS IN THE BLOOD

You fall and scrape your knee at recess. It's red, swollen, hot, and painful. Ouch! Those uncomfortable sensations are normal. They're part of a body response called **inflammation**. The immune system triggers this response to protect the body.

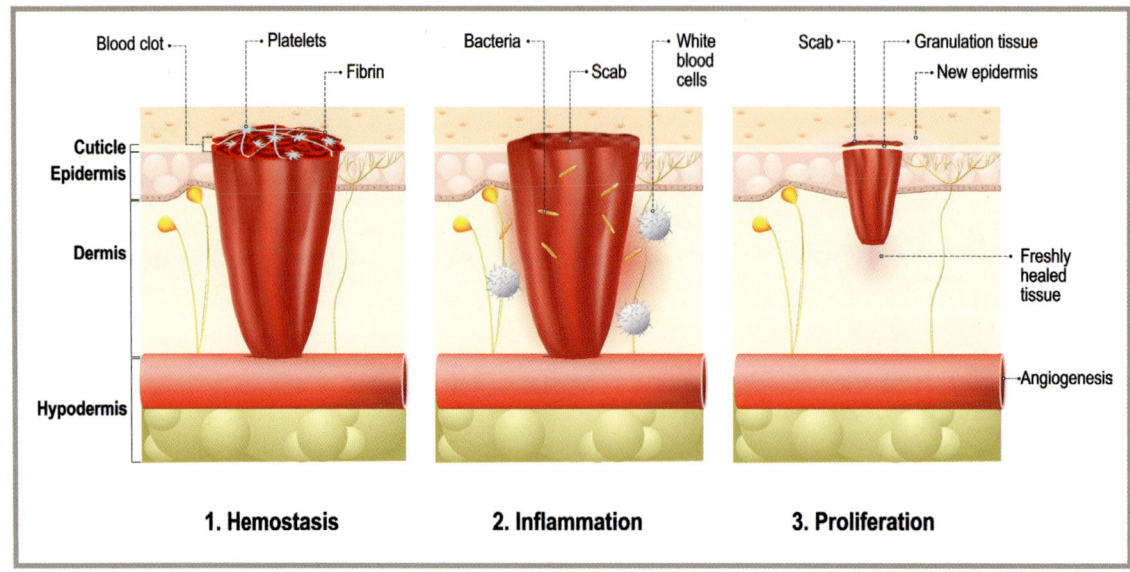

The body responds to an injury in three stages. Hemostasis stops any bleeding. Inflammation sends white blood cells to attack germs. Proliferation builds new, healthy skin.

As the body sends more blood to the injury, the area heats up. It also reddens as the vessels carrying the blood get larger. The vessels release white blood cells. These act like soldiers. They attack germs and other unwanted invaders.

Even the searing pain of an injury has a purpose. You avoid using the hurt area. That helps it heal faster.

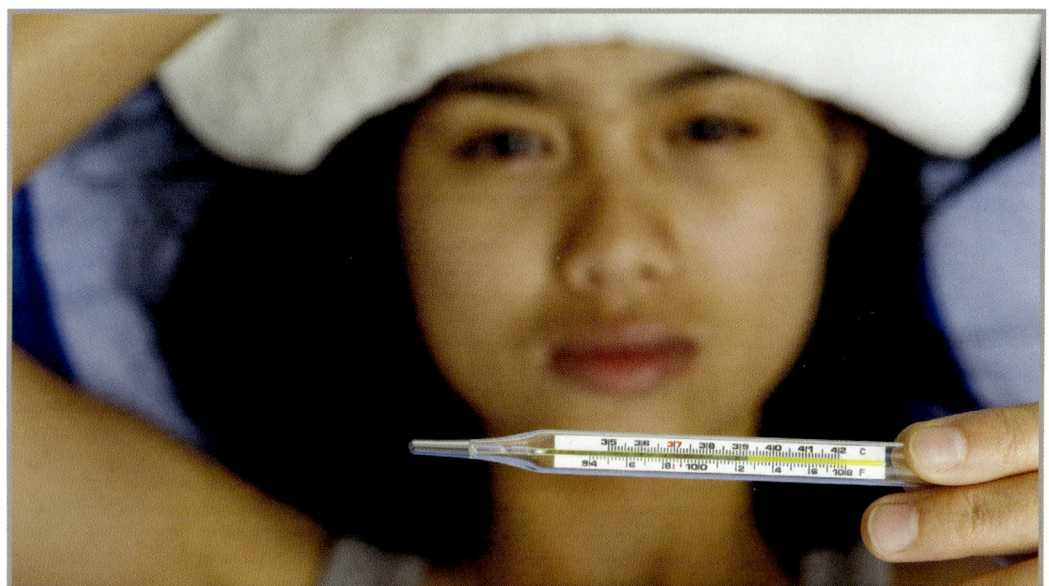

Fever
Sometimes, inflammation leads to a fever. Most germs prefer a normal body temperature. A low fever helps kill germs. It also prompts the immune system to work harder. But a very high fever is dangerous. Medicine can help bring it down.

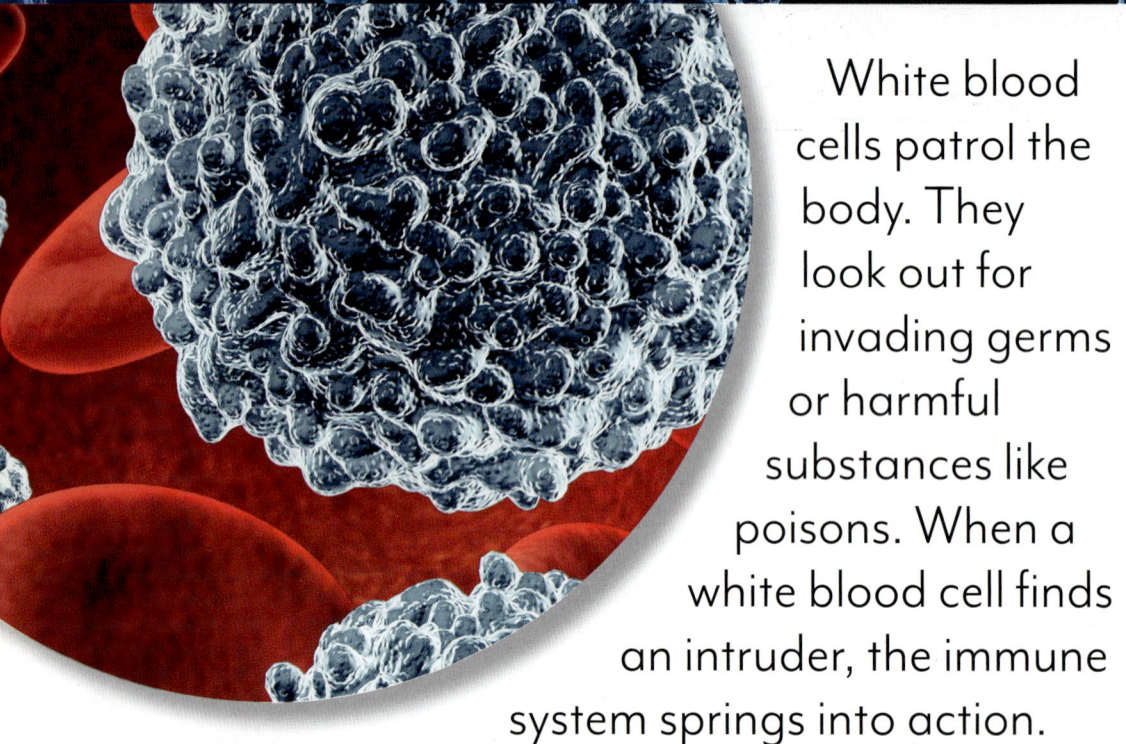

White blood cells patrol the body. They look out for invading germs or harmful substances like poisons. When a white blood cell finds an intruder, the immune system springs into action.

First the immune system learns to recognize the intruder. Then it produces weapons called **antibodies**. These target and destroy that specific intruder. But it takes time to figure out how to make the right weapon. So during a germ's very first attack, you'll likely feel sick.

But the next time that same germ shows up, the immune system remembers what to do. The body's tiny soldiers can fight off the attack before you get sick.

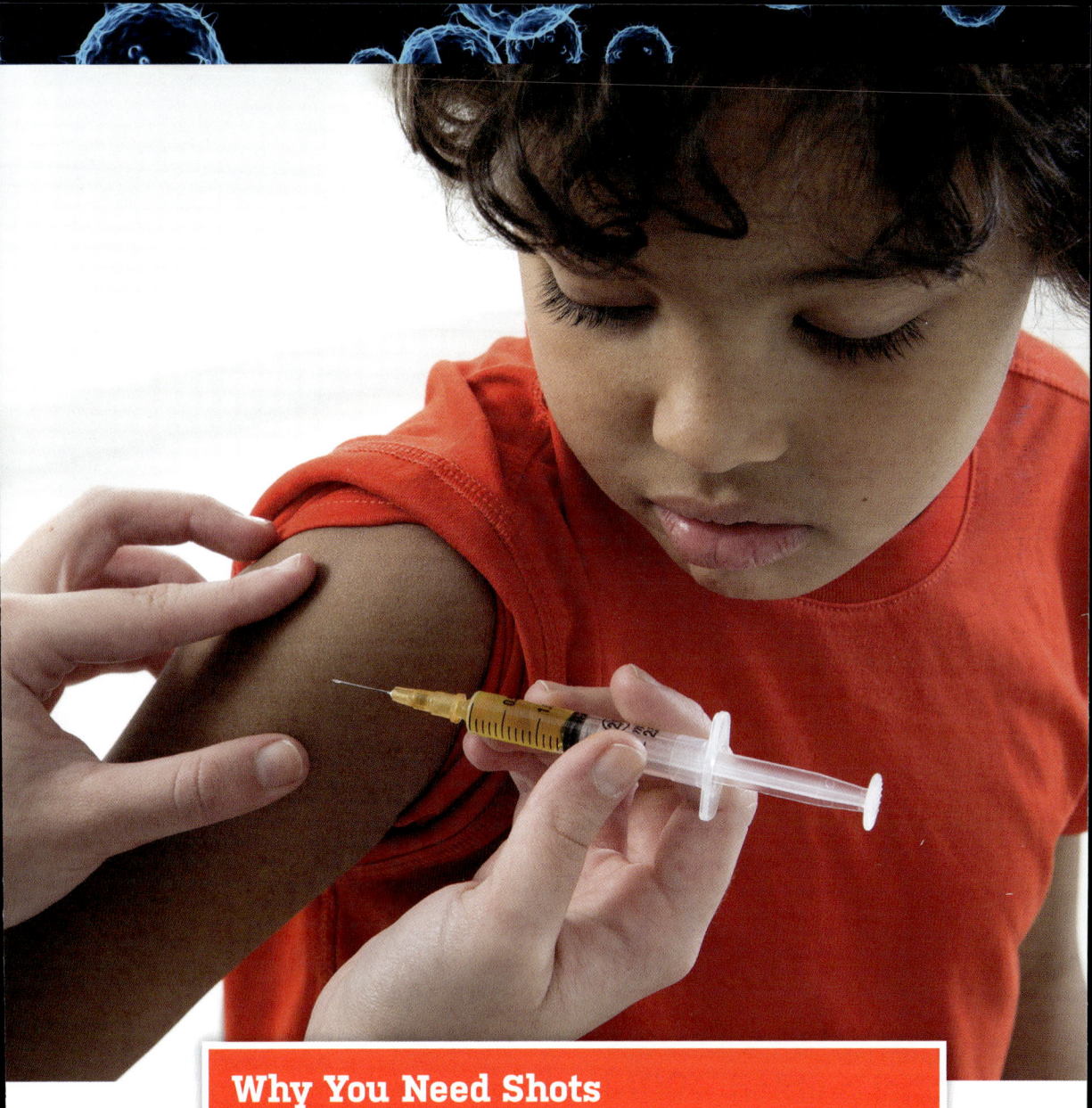

Why You Need Shots
A shot, or vaccine, puts weak germs into the body. These germs can't make you sick. But the body learns to fight them. Then you can't get the disease the germ causes. Thanks to vaccines, kids in most countries around the world no longer get a crippling disease called polio.

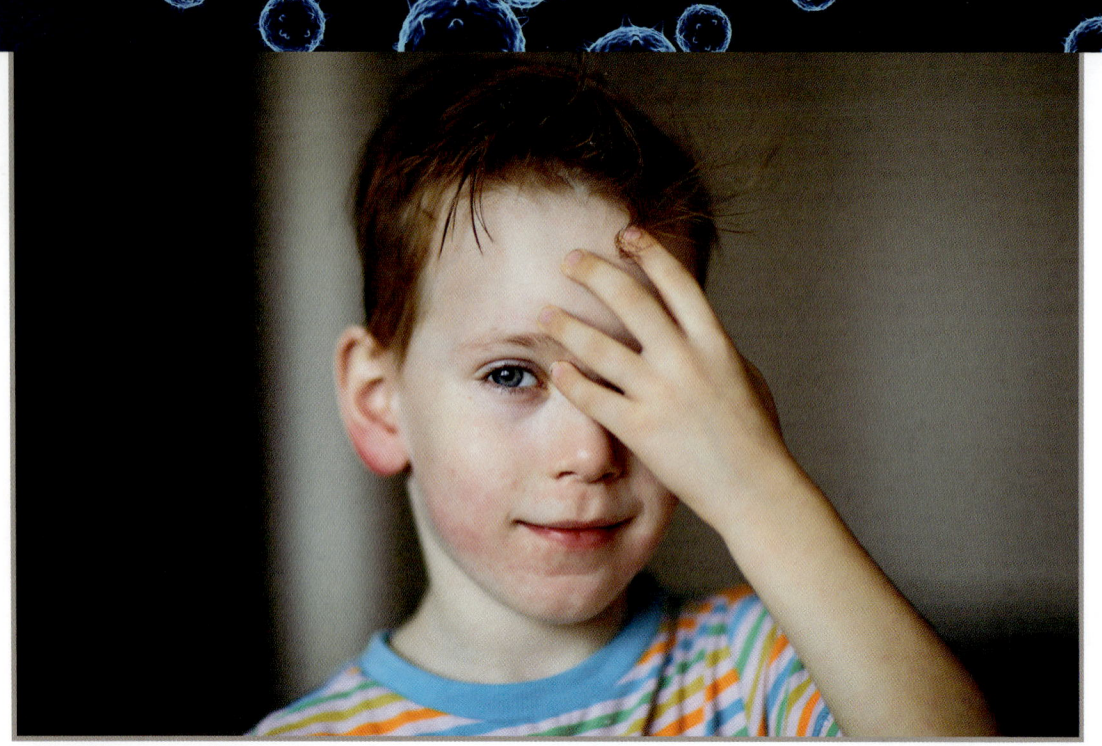
An allergic reaction may cause an itchy rash.

Sometimes the immune system makes mistakes. Its soldiers may attack a substance that isn't normally harmful, such as peanuts or pollen. This type of mistake is called an allergy. An allergy can cause swelling, itching, a rash, or even breathing problems.

The immune system may also target healthy body systems. In one type of arthritis, the body attacks its own fingers, hips, knees, or other joints.

Some diseases weaken the immune system. AIDS is a dangerous illness. A body with AIDS has almost no defense against germs and other invaders.

GOT ALLERGIES?

People with allergies must avoid certain foods, animals, insects, or other substances.

40% — *children in the U.S. with allergies*

3 to 30 minutes — *the amount of time it takes for a severe allergic reaction to occur*

Peanuts Milk — *the most common food allergies*

100 — *the number of people in the U.S who die from bee stings each year*

Coins Jewelry — *the metal nickel gives some people a rash*

AIDS stands for acquired immune deficiency syndrome. It is a disease of the immune system caused by human immunodeficiency virus (HIV). There is no cure for AIDS, but some medications can slow the progress of the disease and help fight **infections**.

MEET THE INVADERS

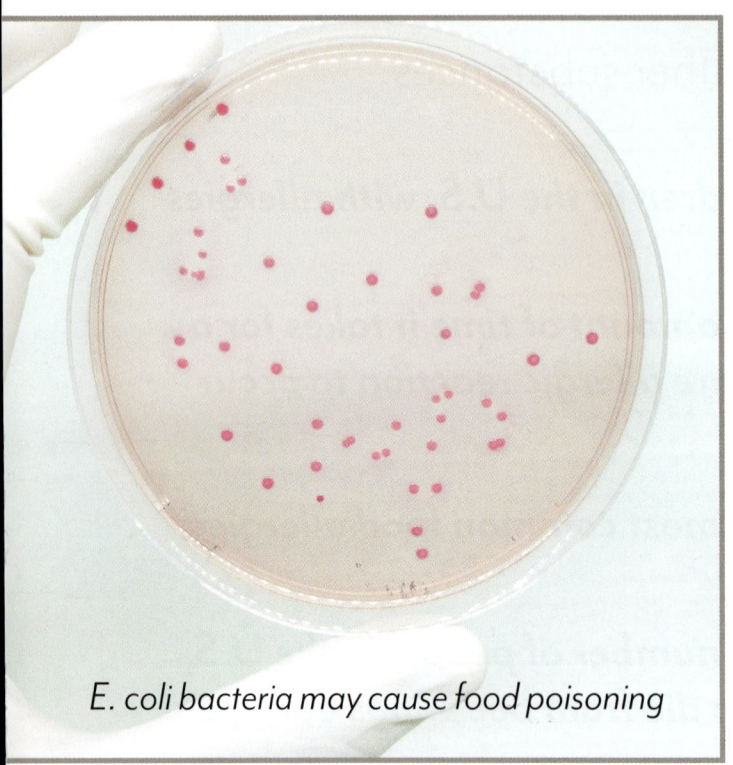

E. coli bacteria may cause food poisoning

Germs surround us at all times. Scientists call them **microbes**. They're so small, you need a microscope to see them! Microbes float in the air. They hide in dirt, water, and food. They set up camp all over our bodies.

Sometimes, microbes multiply in the body and mess with its systems. This is called an infection. A healthy immune system fights infections. But as the battle rages on, a person may feel very sick.

Coughing, sneezing, and a runny nose all expel bad microbes from the body. Vomiting and diarrhea also get rid of stuff the body doesn't want inside.

A GUIDE TO GERMS

Type	Relative Size	Description	Examples of Diseases
Viruses	20 to 400 nanometers	A very tiny particle (not technically alive) that takes over the cells of its host	Common cold, influenza, rabies, Zika, AIDS
Bacteria	200 to 10,000 nanometers	Single-celled living things that are not plants or animals. They come in round, rod-like, and curved shapes	Pneumonia, Lyme disease, most ear infections, most cases of food poisoning
Fungi	2,500 nanometers or larger	A plant relative, including mold and mushrooms	Athlete's foot, yeast infection
Protozoa	Around 50,000 nanometers	Single-celled creatures, including amoebas and algae	Malaria
Parasitic animals	1 million or more nanometers	Small worms and other insects that live on and harm a host body	Lice, tapeworms

Millimeter = 1 Thousandth of a Meter

Nanometer = 1 Billionth of a Meter

Coffee Bean = 12 x 8 million nm

Grain of Rice = 8 x 2.5 million nm

Grain of Salt = 500,000 nm

The germs that make people sick often travel from person to person. A disease that spreads like this is **contagious**. Some microbes only spread in body fluids. Other germs may hitch a ride through the air in a cough or sneeze. Or they may hop from the skin to surfaces people touch. Washing your hands regularly will help stop many harmful germs from spreading.

Insects and animals sometimes infect people with dangerous microbes. Tick bites may contain bacteria that cause Lyme disease. Mosquitoes spread the malaria parasite and the Zika virus.

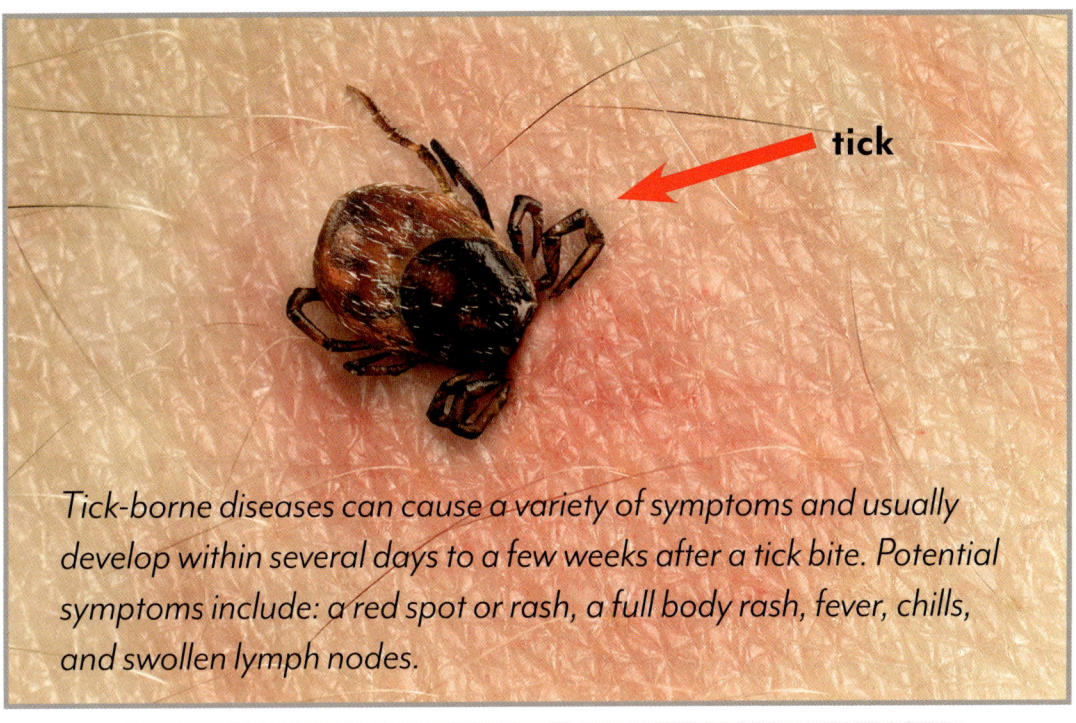

Tick-borne diseases can cause a variety of symptoms and usually develop within several days to a few weeks after a tick bite. Potential symptoms include: a red spot or rash, a full body rash, fever, chills, and swollen lymph nodes.

An Accidental Discovery
Bacteria cause many human diseases. Doctors fight these diseases with medicines called **antibiotics**. The British scientist Alexander Fleming discovered the first antibiotic, penicillin, in 1928. The discovery was an accident: mold grew on one of his experiments. It turned out that the mold could kill harmful bacteria.

HELPFUL MICROBES

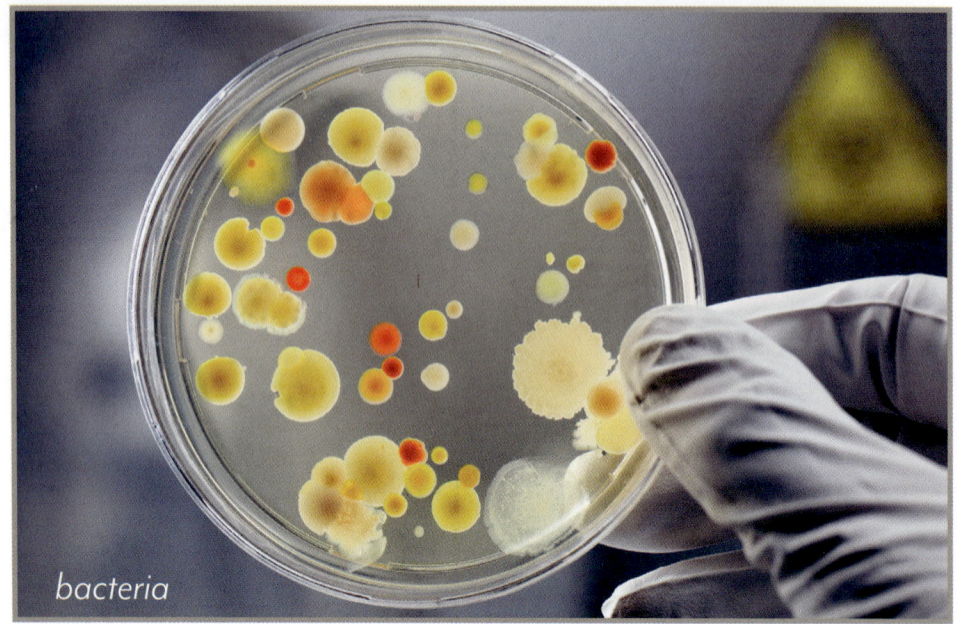

bacteria

Germs may seem scary. But most microbes are harmless. And some help keep you healthy.

Your body contains trillions of microbes. Most are different kinds of bacteria. They live in communities on the skin, in the mouth, and other places. Gut microbes help digest food. They train the immune system. They even make chemicals that affect the brain.

In a healthy community, microbes compete for space. If one type tries to take over, its neighbors keep it in check. If a strange microbe shows up, the community kicks it out. This protects against infection.

Yummy Yogurt
Probiotics help add healthy bacteria to the body. The good bacteria in yogurt and other probiotic foods help fight off bad, disease-causing bacteria. The science of probiotics is still developing.

LIVING A HEALTHY LIFE

Like any machine, the human body needs regular care. Following some simple rules can help people get or stay in tip-top shape: Eat healthy food, drink water, and exercise daily. Get enough sleep and avoid stress.

But not everyone manages to live like this. Many people feel stressed daily. They eat fatty and sugary foods. They don't always exercise. They may smoke or drink alcohol. These people are more likely to get sick. They are also more likely to become overweight. And they face a greater risk of dying from a heart attack or stroke.

HEALTHY HABITS FOR KIDS

6 to 8
glasses of water each day. Replace most fruit juice and soda with water.

Fruit, vegetables, nuts, beans, whole grains
Eat these with every meal.

Cake, cookies, candy, white bread
Eat these only occasionally.

9 to 11
hours of sleep kids should get each night.

1 hour
amount of exercise kids should get each day. Find activities that are fun for you!

Germs, unhealthy food, stress, and more. These threats to the body come from the outside world. But other dangers lurk within. The cells in a person's body each contain a set of instructions, called **genes**. Genes tell cells how to do their jobs. Parents pass their genes on to their children.

Sometimes, genes contain mistakes. A baby may be born with a genetic disorder. For example, hemophilia makes a cut or scrape very dangerous. The body can't stop bleeding.

But that type of genetic disorder is rare. In most cases, genes and lifestyle both matter. They combine to increase the risk for a disorder. These illnesses run in families. Examples include heart disease and breast cancer.

The spiral shape in this child's hands represents a DNA molecule. Each cell in the body contains a full set of genes made from segments of DNA.

Some disorders impact the mind. A problem with mood, thinking, or behavior is called a mental illness. Depression causes such sadness that a person can't perform daily tasks. Eating disorders lead to unhealthy weight gain or weight loss.

A person's life experiences may lead to mental illness. Going through great stress or violence puts a person at risk. But genes matter, too. Scientists are working to identify genes that put people at risk for mental illness.

Addiction and Recovery
Some people can't stop drinking alcohol or taking drugs. This behavior is called an **addiction**. It is a disease, not a choice. Recovery takes time. The person may need to stay at a treatment center.

CANCER

After heart disease, cancer kills the most people in the world each year. But cancer isn't one disease. It's many. In all cancers, some of the body's own cells get damaged. They start to grow out of control. This causes sickness and sometimes death.

What causes cancer? Lots of things. Too much time in the sun without sunscreen may lead to skin cancer. Smoking can cause lung cancer. Getting old increases the risk of cancer. Genes, lifestyle, pollution, and even viruses may also cause cancer.

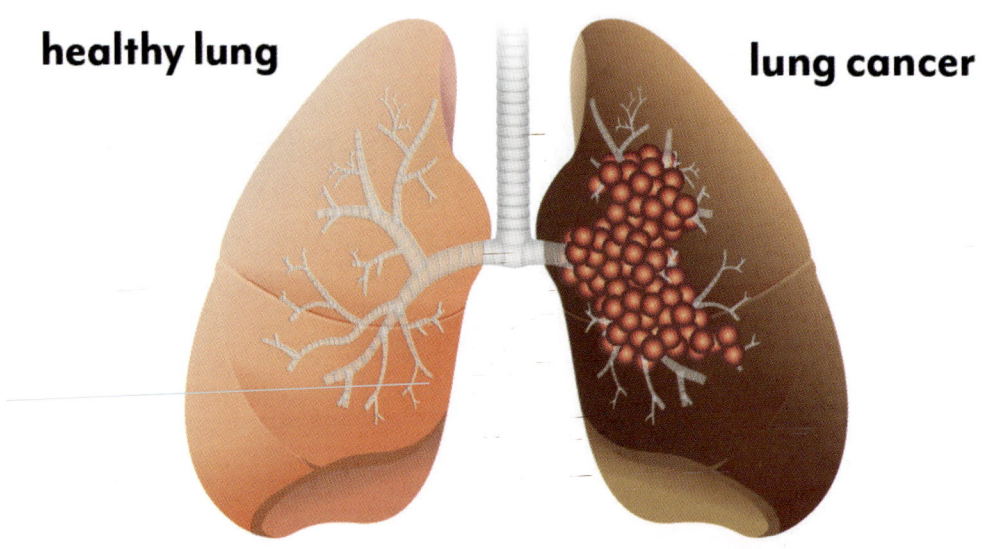

Comparison between a healthy lung and one with cancerous tumors

CANCER MYTHS

Do cell phones or power lines cause cancer?

Does fake sugar cause cancer?

Can herbal medicines treat cancer?

Can a person recover from cancer?

Answers

Do cell phones or power lines cause cancer? No.
Does fake sugar cause cancer? No.
Can herbal medicines treat cancer? No.
Can a person recover from cancer? Yes, many people survive cancer.

The immune system normally seeks and destroys cancer cells. But it doesn't always get them all. And some cancers don't make a person feel sick at first. Doctors regularly check older people for common cancers.

There's no single cure for cancer. But many treatments exist. Surgery can remove a cancerous growth, called a tumor. Powerful light can zap a tumor. Strong medications can also destroy cancer cells.

The body can't last forever. As a person gets older, the machine begins to break down. Death is unavoidable. It's a fact of life. Understanding disease will help people enjoy life for as long as they can.

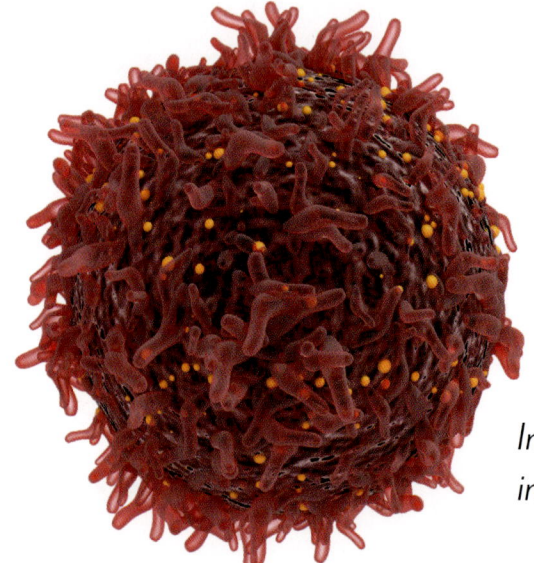

Immunotherapy boosts the body's own immune system to fight cancer cells.

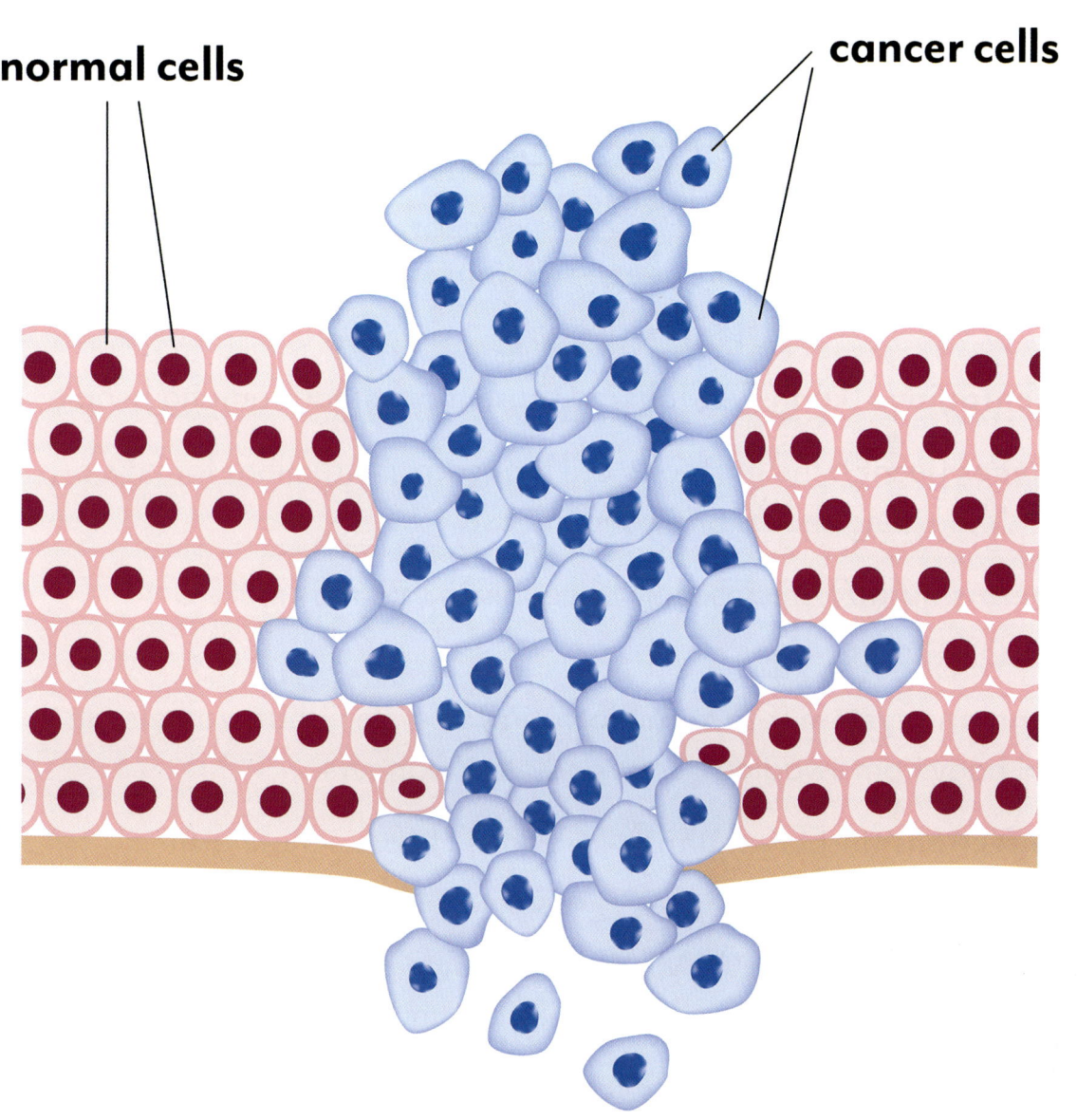

cancer cells in a growing tumor

GLOSSARY

addiction (uh-DIK-shuhn): a consuming need to use alcohol, drugs, or another substance

antibiotics (an-ti-bye-AH-tiks): medications that kill or harm bacteria in order to cure infections

antibodies (AN-ti-bah-deez): substances created by the immune system to target specific threats

contagious (kuhn-TAY-juhs): disease that spreads among people

genes (jeenz): the parts of a cell that carry instructions for how a living thing should grow and behave

germs (jurmz): microscopic living things that may make a person sick

immune system (i-myoon SIS-tuhm): a system that protects the body from invading germs and other dangers

infections (in-FEK-shuhnz): invasions of germs that harm the body

inflammation (in-fluh-MAY-shuhn): a normal body response to injury that involves redness, swelling, and heat

microbes (MYE-krobes): microscopic living things that may be helpful or harmful

probiotics (pro-bye-AH-tiks): foods or medications that introduce helpful bacteria into the body

INDEX

allergies 13
antibiotics 17
cancer 22, 26, 27, 28, 29
diarrhea 14
fever 9
genes 22, 24, 26
germs 4, 5, 6, 9, 10, 11, 12, 14, 15, 16, 18, 22
heart disease 22, 26
immune system 5, 6, 8, 9, 10, 12, 13, 14, 18, 28
infection(s) 13, 14, 15, 17, 18
injury 4, 8, 9
lifestyle 22, 26
mental illness 24
microbes 14, 16, 17, 18
skin 6, 8, 16, 17, 18, 26
vaccines 11
vomiting 14

SHOW WHAT YOU KNOW

1. What are three things the body's immune system does?

2. Why does a scraped knee swell and turn red?

3. Why do some people have allergies?

4. What are five things you can do to keep your body healthy?

5. What do all cancers have in common?

FURTHER READING

Cline-Ransome, Lesa and Ransome, James, *Germs: Fact and Fiction, Friends and Foes*, Henry Holt and Co., 2017.

Latchana Kenney, Karen, *Immune System*, Jump! Inc., 2017.

Midthun, Joseph and Hiti, Samuel, *Fighting Sickness*, World Book, Inc., 2016.

ABOUT THE AUTHOR

Kathryn Hulick decided to write books for kids after returning from two years serving in the Peace Corps in Kyrgyzstan. Her favorite subjects are science and technology. She's written about everything from robots and outer space to dinosaurs. She enjoys hiking, painting, reading, and working in her garden. Learn more about her work at kathrynhulick.com.

Meet The Author!
www.meetREMauthors.com

© 2019 Rourke Educational Media

All rights reserved. No part of this book may be reproduced or utilized in any form or by any means, electronic or mechanical including photocopying, recording, or by any information storage and retrieval system without permission in writing from the publisher.

www.rourkeeducationalmedia.com

PHOTO CREDITS: Cover & Title Pg ©Ugreen, ©Esben_H, Pg 3 to 32 (top bar) ©Rost-9D, Pg 3 ©Ugreen, Pg 4 ©FatCamera, Pg 5 ©FatCamera, Pg 6 ©By solar22, Pg 7 ©VEX Collective, Pg 8 ©By Designua, Pg 9 ©By swissmacky, Pg 10 ©Brain light/Alamy Stock Photo, Pg 11 ©By JPC-PROD, Pg 12 ©By Malochka Mikalai, Pg 13 ©LenaSkor, Pg 14 ©By RUJIPAS YONGSAWAS, Pg 15 ©Ilonalmagine, ©By Hafidzu, Pg 16 ©Valeriy_G, Pg 17 ©By Smileus, Pg 18 ©Andreas Reh, Pg 19 ©chombosan, Pg 20 ©Serg_ Velusceac, Pg 23 ©Steve Debenport, Pg 24 ©bodnarchuk, Pg 25 ©KatarzynaBialasiewicz, Pg 26 ©By solar22, Pg 27 ©ottokalman, Pg 28 ©CIPhotos, Pg 29 ©By Alila Medical Media

Edited by: Keli Sipperley
Cover design by: Rhea Magaro-Wallace
Interior design by: Kathy Walsh

Library of Congress PCN Data

Diseases and Defenses / Kathryn Hulick
(The Human Machine)
ISBN 978-1-64156-438-0 (hard cover)
ISBN 978-1-64156-564-6 (soft cover)
ISBN 978-1-64156-684-1 (e-Book)
Library of Congress Control Number: 2018930467

Rourke Educational Media
Printed in the United States of America,
North Mankato, Minnesota